IMAGES
of America

BRUNSWICK

MAP OF BRUNSWICK

TOWNSHIP 4 N.   RANGE 14 W.

Scale 2½ inches to 1 Mile

No. 8

CUYAHOGA CO.

STRONGSVILLE TP.

LIVERPOOL

HINKLEY

MEDINA

1897

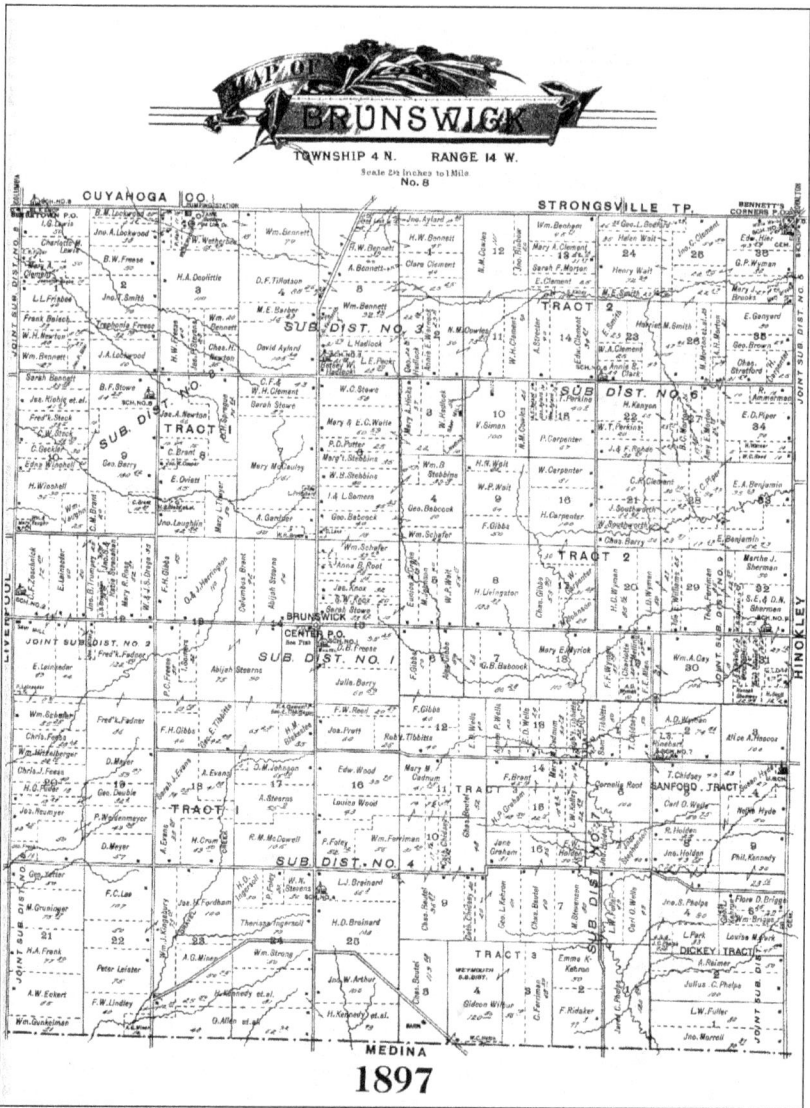

This 1897 map shows Brunswick Township during the time period when most of the photographs included in this book were taken.

(*cover*) In 1903, William S. Harley and Arthur Davidson produced the first Harley-Davidson that was made available to the public. Their first factory was a 10-by-15-foot wooden shed. In 1906, a new factory was built, and there were six full-time employees. The first motorcycle sold for police duty was sold in Detroit, Michigan, in 1908. The Harley-Davidson logo was used for the first time in 1910, and they began to make a mark in racing and endurance tests by winning seven first-place finishes. By 1918, the U.S. military purchased about one-half of all Harley-Davidson motorcycles produced. One day after the signing of the Armistice, the first American to enter Germany was riding a Harley-Davidson. The lure of the Harley-Davidson motorcycle has endured over the last 100-some years. In the 1915 photograph on the cover, the three Brunswick bikers on the left obviously saw the appeal of the Harley-Davidson motorcycle early on. The motorcycle on the right is a Yale, which was manufactured in Toledo, Ohio.

IMAGES
of America

BRUNSWICK

Amber Dalakas with the Brunswick Area Historical Society

ARCADIA
PUBLISHING

Published by Arcadia Publishing
Charleston, South Carolina

Library of Congress Catalog Card Number: 2004107610

For all general information contact Arcadia Publishing at:
Telephone 843-853-2070
Fax 843-853-0044
E-mail sales@arcadiapublishing.com
For customer service and orders:
Toll-Free 1-888-313-2665

Visit us on the Internet at www.arcadiapublishing.com

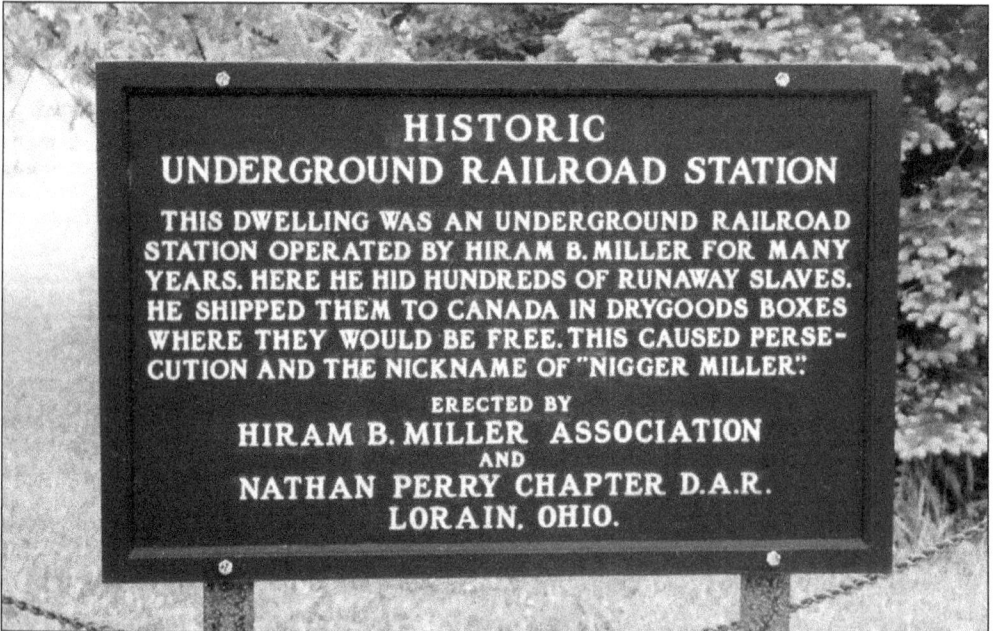

This historic marker on West 130th Street just north of Laurel Road marks one of the major sites on the Underground Railroad. This was the home of Hiram Miller, who moved to this area in 1833 with his family from Monroe County, New York. Hiram helped many slaves escape to Canada. Mr. Miller felt it was his religious duty to help the runaway slaves escape. After the fugitive slave law was enacted, some neighbors tried to find the runaways to claim the $500 reward. However, not one slave who came through his care was captured. Reportedly, Hiram helped more than 1,000 slaves escape toward freedom. (Photograph courtesy of the Fuller family.)

CONTENTS

ACKNOWLEDGMENTS

This book would not have been possible without the help of many people. I would like to thank my husband Jim and my children Jeanne and Jimmy for their patience, support, and encouragement. Thanks to Laura Krutschnitt for her help with the captions. I appreciate the guidance and encouragement that "Sam" Boyer provided. Special thanks to the members of the Brunswick Area Historical Society who have supported and encouraged me; to Ellen Gibbs, our historian, for all of her help and patience and for answering my many questions; and to Mamie Grunau, our president, for her direction and help.

I would like to thank all who shared not only their photographs but their family's history, without which this book would not have been possible. They were: Forrest Keller, Lori Chidsey Wagner, Pat Van Hoose, Ellen Gibbs, Grace Ruf, Walt Wozniak, Bill Eyssen, Jeff Lanphear, Albert Sego, Lucille Faster Widdifield, Rose Carlton Miktuk, June Waite Kroupa, Rob Levandoski, Aqua Neura Witkowski, Brunswick United Methodist Church, Rosemarie Skrletts Beyer, Curt Waite, Cathryn Vaughan Buschow, Ellen Gibbs, Bernice Hemeyer, Louise Varisco, Ethel Hemeyer Waite, Les Fuller and family, Clay Benjamin, Nola Benjamin Lowther, Gary Werner, Tony Capstick, Bennett's Corners Community United Methodist Church, Ward Bouman, and Waite and Son Funeral Homes.

The two previous histories that have been done on Brunswick—*An Outline History of Brunswick, 1815–1965*, done by the Historical Committee of the Brunswick Sesquicentennial, and "Sam" Boyer's *Brunswick: Our Hometown*—were invaluable to me. I'd like to thank those who also assisted me: Jim Hayas, Dave Goodyear, Ron Chidsey, and Linda Scarcella; and thanks to Melissa Basilone, my editor, for her encouragement and help.

Unless otherwise noted, photographs were furnished by the Brunswick Area Historical Society.

Heritage Farm Museum—this is the home of the Brunswick Area Historical Society.

INTRODUCTION

In 1815, settlers began traveling from Connecticut, Massachusetts, and New York to an area known as the Western Reserve, which had been granted to Connecticut by the King of England. It was subsequently sold to investors in 1795. Six investors bought all of Brunswick Township, a total of 15,922 acres for $26,087, or $1.64 per acre.

Families came in search of better land, and purchases were random across the township. There was no central town, just farms. The roads that are now U.S. 42 (Pearl Road) and S.R. 303 (Center Road) became the center, as the churches, general stores, a blacksmith shop, and a stage coach route were located in the area. It was known as Brunswick Center.

We have no photographs of those first settlers, but are indebted to them for establishing the foundation on which Brunswick still rests.

The name for the community was chosen because the residents liked the way it looked when it was written. Brunswick has grown from a strictly farming community into a thriving community of over 40,000 residents. The one-room school has given way to a system of school buildings housing over 7,000 students. The general store has grown into many businesses and restaurants along with an industrial park. The mud roads have given way to Interstate 71, bringing Cleveland and Akron closer. The roads have been paved, making travel easier. The interurban rail line was replaced by the automobile and truck as the community became more mobile. Farms have given way to homes and apartments.

We hope you enjoy our trip down memory lane through photographs, for it has been done with you, the reader, in mind. We are grateful for all who shared. Thank you.

—Mamie Grunau, president
Brunswick Area Historical Society
February 2005

The Brunswick Area Historical Society

The goal of the Brunswick Area Historical Society is to preserve something of the area's heritage so that future generations may know something of past residents' everyday lives.

The Historical Society was officially chartered in 1992 as a non-profit corporation. The first goal was to find a home. At the same time, the City of Brunswick was looking for a property to purchase and preserve. A mid-19th-century farm came on the market, which the City purchased. It consisted of 32.5 acres plus farm buildings. The farmstead was to be used as a home for the Historical Society, with the remainder becoming a city park.

Restoration architects Chambers, Murphy and Burge were hired to oversee the restoration. It is a typical small Ohio farm with all the usual farm buildings still standing. First to be restored was the farmhouse, then the barn, the carriage house / garage, and the equipment shed. Work has been done on the privy, corn crib, milk house, and chicken house. The granary is the next to be restored. During restoration of the barn, a hand-dug, stone-lined well was uncovered. It is spring fed and continues to flow. It is the only evidence of a well found on the farm.

The first family on record was Abram and Sarah (nee Harvey) Berdan. Next were their daughter Rachel and her husband William Pitkin. Then in 1887, the farm was sold to George and Julia (nee Behner) Tibbitts. Peter and Mary (nee Walter) Groening purchased the farm in 1940. The Groening Estate sold the 32.5-acre farm to the City of Brunswick in 1995.

The community has filled the buildings with their treasures for all to see and enjoy. It has been restored to represent the time frame of 1850–1930. Working with the City Parks Department, we welcome school children, Boy Scouts, Girl Scouts, and other groups for programs and tours. We welcome all who wish to take a trip back to a time when almost everyone was a farmer and life was, not easier, but simpler. We have named it Heritage Farm for it is our goal to preserve Brunswick's heritage.

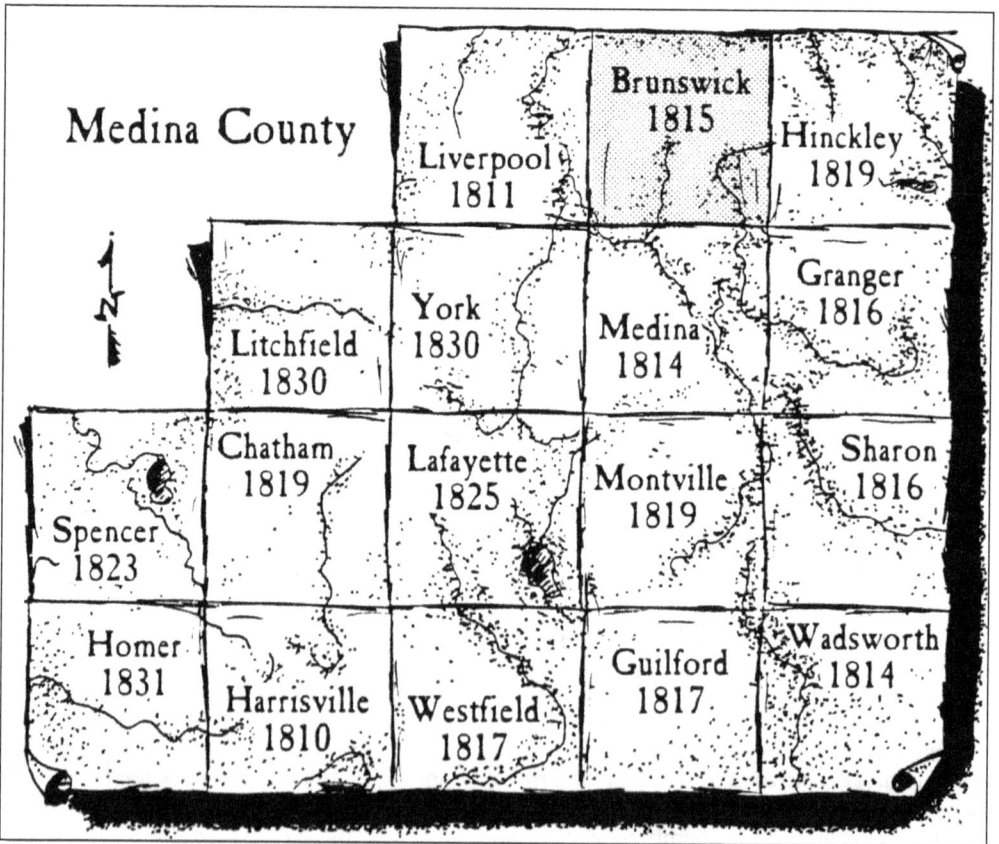

This is the Medina County map with the well-known stair steps. (Photograph courtesy of "Sam" Boyer's *Brunswick: Our Hometown*.)

One

THE COMMUNITY GROWS

The first settlers arrived in Brunswick almost 100 years before this c. 1910 photograph was taken, when there was little more than forest here. This picture shows what was the center of town and the heart of Brunswick, especially for those early settlers. The photo was taken from the bell tower of the Brunswick United Methodist Church, looking northwest. The Westview Cemetery can be seen in the background with the Disciple's Church. The store on the right was owned and operated by the Aylard brothers, Harry and Arthur. During the late 1800s and into the 1900s, Harry and Arthur operated a slaughterhouse near where Conrad's Tires is today. Arthur later became Medina treasurer and his brother Harry a cashier in the Savings Deposit Bank of Medina. The house behind the large tree to the left of the store was that of Dr. Hawkins. Behind the Aylard store was a livery stable.

Pictured here are the Brunswick Post Office and the Aylard Brothers' Store, owned and operated by Harry and Arthur Aylard. Rural Free Delivery began here about 1904. The first experimental rural free delivery took place in West Virginia in 1896. Rural free delivery was initiated to provide farmers with free mail delivery and services so that they wouldn't have to travel into town. The mail carrier provided his own horse, buggy, feed, and water and was paid $45 per month. Rural free delivery spurred the development and improvement of America's roads and highways. Brunswick's first mail carriers were Lewis Peck, Theo Chapman, and Fred Usher, who is pictured with his son here c. 1907, as they head off on deliveries. The store was located on the southwest corner of Pearl and Center Roads.

Walter Folley is pictured here c. 1910, with his team of horses and wagon. He was the local butcher who worked at the Aylard Brothers' Store.

This is the Usher & Waite General Store and Brunswick Post Office *c.* 1909–1912. The building is located on the southwest corner of Routes 303 and 42 and is still in use today. The bricks from the Congregational Church that was at one time on the northeast corner of the intersection were used to build this building in the early 1900s. The store was on the left and the post office on the right. Shown here are left to right: Harry Vaughn, Walter Folley, Lewis Peck and his son Herbert (the mail carriers in the doorway), and Harv Myrick with his back to the camera.

The Usher & Waite grocery wagon was used to deliver meat and groceries throughout the area.

This c. 1916 photograph shows Brunswick Circle, with the view looking south and the Brunswick United Methodist Church in the background.

The Brunswick Circle is seen here c. 1910, with the view looking south.

According to *An Outline History of Brunswick*, the Brunswick Circle (pictured here *c.* 1907) began as little more than swampy land with a wooden bridge across it. It was then made into a circle and later gave way to the Federal Highway Department (p. 23). "The fast colts of this community are brought to this new park and their speed and action exhibited to a fine audience."

Bill and Jim are the horses pulling the carriage in front of the Babcock Store. The house in back of the store is where Sarah (nee Sherman) and George Byron Babcock first lived. Sarah is one of the folks standing in the doorway. Stephen and Dell Babcock are seated in the front wagon, which was used to transport goods from station to store. (Photograph courtesy of Jeff Lanphear.)

13

The Pritchard & Livingston General Store was located on the southeast corner of Routes 303 and 42. Jay Livingston is pictured below in the wagon. The Independent Order of Odd Fellows (IOOF) Hall was upstairs. This building burned down in 1911 and was rebuilt in brick. In succeeding years, businesses located here included: Perkins & Ridiker, Benjamin & Leinseder, Babcock's, Zimmerman's, and, finally, Bishop Realty. (Photograph courtesy of Forrest Keller.)

This is the Perkins and Ridiker General Store c. 1912, one of the businesses located in the building on the southeast corner of Routes 303 and 42. Shown in the top photograph are Ora Ridiker and Morris Perkins inside the store at the counter. Zimmerman's store was later located here, and the last business located here before the building was demolished in 1984 was Bishop Realty.

The Bishop Realty building located on the southeast corner of Routes 303 and 42 is seen here on June 5, 1984, shortly before it was demolished. (Photograph courtesy of Forrest Keller.)

In the spring of 1900, northbound travelers on Route 42 would see this view of the Brunswick Center. The Frank Babcock home is on the left where First Merit Bank stands today. The Congregational Church is in the right forefront, with the Byron Babcock home in the right background. The chain was strung around the circle, to mark the path where horses and buggies traveled.

16

This is the Brunswick Circle as it looked in 1932 facing northeast towards the First Christian Church. (Photograph courtesy of Forrest Keller.)

This c. 1910 photograph was taken from the Center Primary School, located on Pearl Road, north of Route 303, looking east from the schoolhouse. Second from the right in the back row is Alvin Gibbs. Jake Keller's home can be seen in the background.

The Brunswick High School/Town Hall, built in 1891, was located on Route 42 just south of the Methodist Church. The interior during a musical program is pictured below c. 1913–1914. Community functions, such as school plays, dances, lectures, musical programs, and grange and town meetings, were held here up until 1925. The auditorium was built at this time in the south house of what is today's Edwards Middle School. The Old Town Hall was demolished in 1976 after a new city hall complex was built on Route 303, completed in 1974. (Photograph courtesy of Jeff Lanphear.)

The Wooster Pike Garage was owned by C. Miner. Originally a blacksmith shop, this building was located on the southwest corner of Route 303 and Route 42. It was home to several other businesses, including a store that was owned by C.H. Anderson and C. Zimmerman, as well as Jimone Garage, Carlton Garage, Arthur Mellert Garage, and Gray's Pumps. Around 1924, gasoline dripped down into the grease pit and onto a light bulb, where it caught fire and caused the building to burn down. (Photograph courtesy of Forrest Keller.)

This is what Midas Muffler looked like c. 1938 when it was Carlton Brothers Ford and Garage, which was owned by brothers Corte and Blake Carlton. Corte Carlton bought the building, which was the Arthur Mellert Garage in 1924, and was joined by his brother Blake in 1925. Together, they opened the Ford dealership that operated here for 27 years. (Photograph courtesy of Rose Carlton Miktuk.)

The Old Town Hall is on the left, next to the barn and home that originally belonged to Isaac and Almeda Ward in the 1870s. At the time this photograph was taken in 1918, the home was owned by Frank Case. Today, Walt's Restaurant and Brunswick Floral Company and Gifts are located at this site on Route 42, which at the time of this photograph was little more than a mud road. The barn (pictured in the middle) is still standing today but has been moved to just north of Walt's Pizza, behind Stu's Dry Cleaners.

Route 42 South is seen here as it appeared in the mid-1940s. Today, Walt's Pizza and Brunswick Floral Company and Gifts are located in the home on the right. You can see the Village Tavern, which was owned by Tom and Irene Hogue. Their children are Bill Hogue and Dorie Reed of Medina. The restaurant was later owned by Jennie Harblaugh. (Photograph courtesy of Rose Carlton Miktuk.)

20

This building was originally Carr's Carriage and Wagon Shop, dating back to 1845. When this photograph was taken, it was the Morris M. Perkins residence on Pearl Road. Today, the bank across from Edwards Middle School is located there.

Mapleside Farms is seen in this photograph as it looked in the 1940s. (Photograph courtesy of Bill Eyssen.)

This view shows South Street, as Route 42 was known, looking north towards the circle, and Route 303 when it was just a one-lane mud road. This is now Brunswick Plaza, across the street from Edwards and Visintainer Middle Schools.

This view is of Route 42 looking north. John and Betty Dinda owned the home on the left. John Dinda, former mayor, was serving his term when Brunswick became a city on October 2, 1960.

The northwest corner of Routes 303 and 42 is seen here c. 1959. The Babcock house was torn down to make way for Old Phoenix National Bank, seen here. This building was torn down and rebuilt in the 1990s. (Photograph courtesy of Rose Carlton Miktuk.)

This is the northeast corner of the Brunswick Center, as it was prior to much of the Center Road development. The First Christian Church is seen here on the left and Dr. Rodolfo F. Fasoli's house is on the right. In this photograph, the maples that lined Route 303 can be seen. (Photograph courtesy of Rose Carlton Miktuk.)

Looking south in the early 1900s on West 130th Street, at Bennett's Corners, one would see this view of a store and the Methodist Church. The foreground of the photograph shows the watering trough and pump that stood in the middle of the intersection. At this time, West 130th Street, or Town Line Road as it was known then, stopped at Boston Road instead of continuing into Cleveland. The road was paved around 1920. The house on the left belonged to the Meacham family. South of the Meacham house is Perkins and Ridiker General Store. Only the Bennett's Corners Community Methodist Church is still standing today. (Photograph courtesy of Forrest Keller.)

Pictured here is the Levandoski family store and gas station as it looked in the 1920s and 1930s. Ruby (nee Warner) and Rody Levandoski operated the general store from 1919 until 1955. It remained a store through 1976. In 1976, Nick Sidotti purchased the building from the Levandoski family and opened Prima Pizza. The old store was torn down on St. Patrick's Day of 1996 to make way for the West 130th Road widening and intersection renovation. Bennett's Corners was changed forever—no longer did six roads converge at the intersection. Bennett Road and Hunt Road were moved to intersect West 130th north of Bennett's Corners. (Photograph courtesy of Rob Levandoski.)

This is the wedding photograph of Ruby Warner and Rody Levandoski, taken in 1910. (Photograph courtesy of Rob Levandoski.)

George Taylor (standing) and Bert Keller are at the store at Beebetown, which burned down about 1917. It was located on the southwest corner of Marks and Boston Roads in Liverpool Township. The old well stone can still be seen today. (Photograph courtesy of Forrest Keller.)

This is the view you would have seen in the 1920s if you were looking south towards Route 303 on Substation Road. The white block sat in front of the Neura home. (Photograph courtesy of Aqua Neura Witkowski.)

Althea and Kathryn Vaughan are seen here with their mother Calla (nee Gibbs) c. 1920. Their farm was located at present day Diana Drive and Center Road. The maples that lined both sides of Route 303 can be seen in front of their home. (Photograph courtesy of Kathryn Buschow.)

This is the view that you would have seen from Town Line Road (West 130th Street) in 1907 at the Fuller Farm. Cattle were raised for beef on the farm and various crops were cultivated. (Photograph courtesy of the Fuller family.)

This aerial view shows the Waite Farm in the early 1960s, before Interstate 71 was built and the farm was divided in half. Many generations of farmers in the Waite family have raised chickens, sheep, and pigs, and crops produced on the farm include sweet corn, field corn, soy beans, hay, and oats. The Waites settled here over 150 years ago, and the farm is one of the last remaining in Brunswick. However, it too has recently been sold for development. Looking south with North Carpenter along the right, the Rose mansion can be seen in the upper left hand corner along Grafton Road. The Rose property will soon be the new Rosewood Development. (Photograph courtesy of Curt Waite.)

Seen here is construction of Interstate 71 during the summer of 1964. The completion of Interstate 71 on April 1, 1974 brought the "city" to Brunswick and the building boom began. (Photograph courtesy of June Waite Kroupa.)

This is the Ruf farm before it was developed into Old Mill Village in 1970. (Photograph courtesy of Grace Ruf.)

The Brunswick Plaza was built by John Dinda in 1955 and is seen here c. 1957, shortly after it opened. The bowling alley was built at this time as well. (Photograph courtesy of Clay Benjamin.)

This is an early view, c. 1950s, of Laurel Square Shopping Center, which opened in 1959 and was formerly known as Pratt's Pasture.

Forrest and Lillian (nee Gibbs) Myrick owned the Brunswick Lake property around the turn of the last century. (Photograph courtesy of Ellen Gibbs.)

Henry Faster is pictured here plowing at his home on Keller Drive. During the Depression, he lived in Cleveland, where it was difficult to find work and provide for his family. He began buying day-old bread from the bakeries in Cleveland and delivering them to the farmers in Brunswick. During his trips to Brunswick, he came to know Dr. Sindelar, who owned the Brunswick Lake property. A deal was worked out, and Henry was able to move his family to the home on the property rent-free in exchange for their becoming caretakers of the property. The Faster family moved to Brunswick in December of 1929. During the time the Faster family lived there, Henry and another gentleman rented a team of horses from Wooster and dug and cleaned out the lake. Once this was accomplished, it became a popular swimming spot for the children and teens of Brunswick. Henry also served as a Brunswick Township zoning inspector in the late 1950s and early 1960s. (Photograph courtesy of Lucille Faster Widdifield.)

This postcard shows an aerial view of Brunswick Lake around 1970, about the time that Old Mill Village was being developed. The east house of the high school had just opened, in 1967. At this time, high school football games were played at what today is Edwards Middle School. Kirsch Stadium was completed in 1976. The first game played in the new stadium ended in Brunswick beating North Royalton 22-12 in a record-breaking year of nine wins and only one loss (to Massilon-Jackson). (Postcard courtesy of Barb Ortiz.)

Seen in the c. 2004 photograph above is an aerial view of Brunswick Lake, showing the culmination of years of thought, planning, and development. The Kalfas family owned the property for many years. Negotiations began in 1997, and the 107-acre property, which included the 14-acre lake, transferred to the City of Brunswick in 1998. The planning process began with the formation of the Brunswick Lake Steering Committee, who worked with consultants retained by the city. The committee consisted of representatives from local businesses, city government, churches, schools, and residents. The Zaremba Company was chosen as the developer for the project in 2000. In early 2001, the city acquired 36 acres immediately east of the Brunswick Lake property, and it was incorporated into the master plan. Planning continued through 2003. May 16th, 2003 marked the groundbreaking ceremony, the construction phase beginning. Home Depot was the first store to be completed, opening in January of 2004. Many businesses have been added since that time, as the property continues to be developed. (Above, photograph courtesy of Gary Werner; below, photograph courtesy of Anthony Capstick, City of Brunswick.)

Two

GETTING AROUND
AND GETTING BY

Almost 100 years after the settlers arrived in Brunswick, the first pavement was laid. This photograph shows the process of laying the first brick pavement in 1915. These men are paving Route 303 east, which was one lane only. The beautiful maple trees that lined both sides of Route 303 can be seen in this photograph.

There were many modes of transportation in the early days of Brunswick. Looking northeast at the center, oxen are seen pulling a sled c. 1914.

Before automobiles arrived in Brunswick, horses and buggies were used to get around. Bert and Bernice (nee Freese) Keller are pictured in their buggy. In the early days, it would take two and a half to three days to make a trip to Cleveland. (Photograph courtesy of Forrest Keller.)

In the top photograph, looking northwest, is the Brunswick traffic circle at the intersection of Routes 303 and 42. The Babcock house is the large white house in the background. The grader in the foreground was used to clear the roads of snow, dust, and mud. It was pulled by a team of horses. Whoever was traveling north would drag the grader as far as they were traveling. The next person heading south would pull it back. The photograph below shows Bert Keller and Arthur Buschman scraping roads so that the "kid wagon," as the early school buses were called, could deliver the children to school, and so that others could easily travel through the township. (Above, photograph courtesy of Forrest Keller; below, photograph courtesy of Forrest Keller.)

Here, Stephen Sherman and Sarah Selena Sherman are pictured in their carriage. (Photograph courtesy of Jeff Lanphear.)

This is a forerunner of the tractor-trailer.

Even though it was a simpler time, life on a Brunswick farm wasn't easy. Any water that was needed for the kitchen or livestock had to be pumped from a well, like the one seen in this photograph of the Fuller Farm. (Photograph courtesy of the Fuller family.)

Karl Ruf is seen working on the Ruf Farm, which was on the west side of North Carpenter Road where the Old Mill Village development is today. (Photograph courtesy of Grace Ruf.)

This photograph is of the Harrington Poultry Club in 1916: (first row) Clyde Freese, Frank Reutter, and unidentified; (second row) Ray Brandt, Morris Case, Handy Miner, and Jack Gavlak; and (third row) Dick Reutter, Howard Chapman, Walter Harrington, Clarance Rohde, and Roy Betsicover.

The Cider Mill was located on Hadcock Road, formerly known as Cider Mill Road, where the Hadlock family lived. The Cider Mill was torn down in the last few years.

Forrest Keller and Elbridge Moxley are seen helping out at the Keller farm. (Photograph courtesy of Forrest Keller.)

This building is a creamery and was located where Wolff's Animal Hospital was, just west of where Ar-Kay Florist is today. The creamery was still functioning at the turn of the last century.

Horses were a way of life in Brunswick for many years. Bert Keller is seen here with a breaking cart, which was used for taming horses. (Photograph courtesy of Forrest Keller.)

The first telephone exchange office, pictured here c. 1913, was located at 1410 Pearl Road and was also the home of E.F. Wyman. Dennis M. Johnson was the first telephone manager, a position he held for 40 years. Not only was Mr. Johnson the manager, he was also the installer and repairman. In 1899, the first toll line between Cleveland and Brunswick was established. Two years later, local lines were installed from Brunswick to the Valley City B&O depot. Residents were then able to find out if their goods had arrived. Other owners of this house have included Morris Perkins, Marie Carleton, Dorothy Leyda, and Marion Wolff. Mrs. Oehlauf and Mrs. Wyman were among the early telephone operators, and Marie (nee Waite) Barabas Fasoli was one of the last.

Horatio Chidsey is seen on the Benjamin Farm feeding the sheep. (Photograph courtesy of the Benjamin family.)

Theo Chapman, his daughter Myrtle Chapman (standing), and an unidentified neighbor girl pose in the Chapman truck, which was packed and ready to go to town to the market. This picture was taken in 1916 at the Chapman Farm, which was located on the north side of Route 303 where Arby's and the Brunswick High School stand today. (Photograph courtesy of Grace Ruf.)

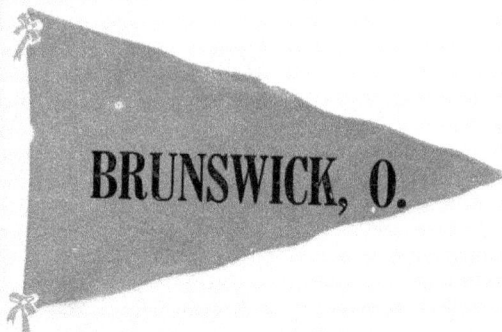

Lookout for the fellows at

BRUNSWICK, O.

You have to kiss or get out and walk.

This is an early Brunswick postcard.

Harmon Babcock's car is pictured here; it was one of the first in Brunswick. Seated in the front seat is Sarah Sherman; in the back are Frank and Carrie Babcock. (Photograph courtesy of Forrest Keller.)

Maple sugar was collected at the Eyssen Farm in the 1930s. (Photograph courtesy of Bill Eyssen.)

The Waite Sugar House was located in the woods on the east side of Interstate 71. Construction of Interstate 71 cut through the middle of the Waite Farm in the early 1960s. The Sugar House was in use through the mid 1940s. (Photograph courtesy of June Waite Kroupa.)

Here, the fields at the Benjamin Farm are being worked. Note the steam tractor in the background. (Photograph courtesy of the Benjamin family.)

About 1913, Farnum H. Gibbs and his son-in-law Harry Lincoln entered into a partnership and established Gibbs & Lincoln Grain and Feed Store. They built this building, which is still standing today; it is located on 303 just east of Substation on the north side of the road. Items sold at their store included: coal, feed, lumber, farm implements, and other supplies. There were two apartments upstairs. Lumber to build this building, as well as the addition in the First Christian Church, was taken from a church that was torn down in Strongsville. This photograph was taken in 1914 shortly after the store opened. The interurban station can be seen to the left on Substation Road.

In this simpler time, before television intruded into our lives in the 20th century, music played a large part in family life. Constance Babcock (Smith) is at the piano, with brother Harmon and their parents, Sarah (nee Sherman) and George Byron Babcock. (Photograph courtesy of Jeff Lanphear.)

Wildlife was plentiful in the early days of Brunswick, and hunting was a necessary way of life. Earl Fuller, pictured in the middle, takes a break while hunting. (Photograph courtesy of the Fuller family.)

The stone quarry was on Laurel Road, west of Route 42. A spur from the interurban train ran from Substation Road to the quarry. (Photograph courtesy of Jeff Lanphear.)

The Cleveland Southwestern Interurban provided freight and passenger service, delivering mail, milk, lumber, coal, bread, and other products. The interurban supplied service from Cleveland, south to Mansfield and Bucyrus. There was generally a two-man crew per car, a motorman, and a conductor, with possibly a second conductor for a trailer. Freight trains might have had a brakeman as it was difficult to do switching with only one man on the ground. For economic purposes, most lines were single track. There were frequent turnouts that allowed the cars to meet and pass. Each stop had a telephone booth for contacting the dispatcher who was at a central location, as many of the stations were unmanned. The telephone was essential to the interurban's operation.

This was the pumping station for the Buckeye Pipe Line. The tracks of the Southwestern Interurban line are in the foreground, with a platform where farmers left their milk for pickup to be taken to the city. Before the interurban line started coming through Brunswick, coal was hauled with horses from Vigil (present-day Strongsville). The coal was used for the steam boilers. The arrival of the interurban allowed coal to be pushed from Vigil to the station coalhouse, ready for use.

Though rail lines sped travel to Cleveland and other cities, there were many wrecks and casualties. Seen here is a collision of the interurban at Strosaker's curve on December 29, 1916.

Ro Moxley was the Brunswick interurban stationmaster. He is pictured here with his dog and gun.

The Brunswick substation, located on the northeast corner of Route 303 and Substation Road, faced west.

This is a c. 1930 rear view of the Southwestern Interurban Station, located at the corner of Route 303 and Substation Road. The children in the wagon are unidentified.

Here, passengers wait for the interurban at the Boston Station.

This photograph shows the Buckeye Pipe Line pumping station.

Mr. and Mrs. P.A. Winkle are pictured here. Mr. Winkle was the superintendent of the pumping station for the Buckeye Pipe Line at Boston and Prospect Roads.

Buckeye Pipe Line Company, a subsidiary of the old Standard Oil Trust, began operations in the pipe line business in 1886 to transport crude oil from the Lima area to refiners on Lake Erie. Twenty acres of land on the southeast corner of Boston and Prospect Roads was purchased in 1890 for the Buckeye Pipe Line's pumping station.

Shown here, the pond on the Buckeye Pipe Line pumping station was built to supply water for the steam engines. The company built five houses on the pond to house their employees; they were torn down once they were no longer needed. The management granted permission for adults and children to use the pond for ice-skating as long as a responsible person was on hand to ensure that there was no smoking close to the highly combustible oil.

Many different types of livestock were raised in the Brunswick area over the last two centuries. Farming has provided an ample living to the people of Brunswick in spite of hard times and the hard work involved. Steve Skrletts is butchering a hog at their farm on North Carpenter Road. (Photograph courtesy of Rosemarie Skrletts Beyer.)

Mamie Waite is cleaning the milking utensils with her daughter June. (Photograph courtesy of June Waite Kroupa.)

Karl Ruf, on the right, brings home dinner. (Photograph courtesy of Grace Ruf.)

Gilbert Fuller is pictured on the left. He must have had a successful outing—note the many coon skins. (Photograph courtesy of the Fuller family.)

Looking northwest at the center *c.* 1914, the Disciples Church is seen in the background at Westview Cemetery, before it was moved to the Brunswick Center. Oxen are pulling a sleigh. (Photograph courtesy of Forrest Keller.)

Pictured at some time during the 1950s, Myron Chidsey is working in a wheat field on the farm of Alwin Wolff, who would later become mayor.

Cows, chickens, and hogs were raised on the Skrletts Farm on North Carpenter Road. (Photograph courtesy of Rosemarie Skrletts Beyer.)

Pictured here is the Skrletts family making sausage, from left to right: Steve Skrletts, Donna Timko, Joe Skrletts, Ann Timko, and Ruth Skrletts. (Photograph courtesy of Rosemarie Skrletts Beyer.)

Brunswick Airport was located on Substation just south of Boston Road on the west side of the road. Hazel and William Morton are in the front seat of the car with Jerry Bitting in the back seat. (Photograph courtesy of Forrest Keller.)

Earle and Winifred Gibbs are enjoying a sleigh ride in the snow.

North Carpenter Road is pictured here during the winter of 1944–1945. Snow began falling on December 11, 1944, and with continual snowstorms throughout the winter, the grass wasn't seen again until February 22, 1945. (Photograph courtesy of June Waite Kroupa.)

Ring-necked pheasants were introduced to Ohio in 1896. The state began stocking pheasants in 1919. The grassy areas here were favorable to the pheasant, and their populations grew, peaking in the 1930s and 1940s with five million birds in the state. Farming procedures changed, and the grassy areas grew smaller and smaller, limiting the pheasant's habitat. Ninety-six percent of the pheasant population was gone by 1978. Various conservation programs have helped rebuild the pheasant population in Ohio, and their numbers are still growing. Gilbert Fuller is seen here with a pheasant for dinner. (Photograph courtesy of the Fuller family.)

Neura's Grove, owned and operated by the Neura family, hosted many gatherings, including family reunions, political rallies, weddings, and church picnics. (Photograph courtesy of Aqua Neura Witkowski.)

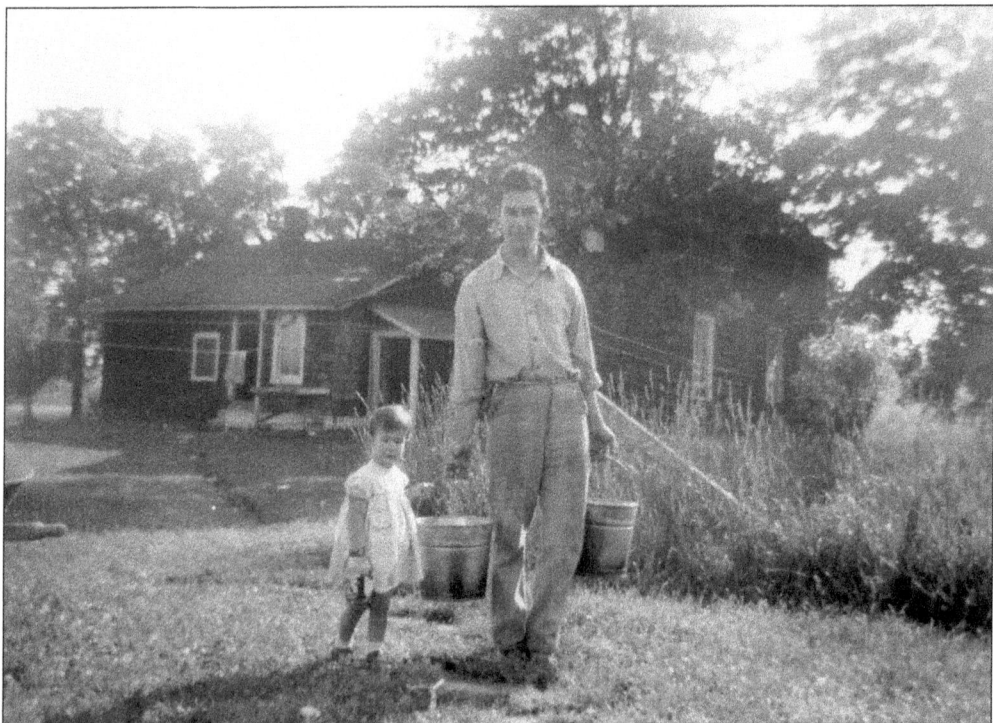

Each member of the family was involved in life on the farm. Steve Skrletts and daughter Rosemarie are hauling water to the livestock at their farm on North Carpenter. (Photograph courtesy of Rosemarie Skrletts Beyer.)

Three

CHURCHES

The Brunswick United Methodist Church is located on the southeast corner of Routes 303 and 42. Formed in 1817 by the Reverend Jacob Ward, it was the first church formed in Brunswick. It is one of the oldest churches in Medina County and the Western Reserve. The church was built in 1872 at a cost of $10,000, which included the land, the building, and the furnishings. Prior to construction, a three-year campaign raised the money needed to build the new church. This photograph shows the church after being remodeled in 1916; the center front entrance was moved to the new bell tower (note the patch on the roof from where the bell tower was removed). Horse and buggy sheds can be seen in the rear. Two stained glass windows from the Congregational Church were installed at this time and are still in place in the sanctuary today. Many changes and additions have been made to the church, with the newest addition completed in 2002. (Photograph courtesy of Brunswick United Methodist Church.)

The interior of the Methodist Church is pictured. (Photograph courtesy of June Waite Kroupa.)

Here is the Brunswick United Methodist Church, located at the southeast corner of Routes 303, as it originally looked. (Photograph courtesy of Jeff Lanphear.)

The Brunswick Methodist Episcopal Church in Westview Cemetery, above, was built in 1830. Four families who came from Pompey, New York, organized the congregation of the Disciples Church in 1835. They met at numerous locations until 1876, when the Disciples Church or First Christian Church purchased the building and the land from the Brunswick United Methodist Church. When the Congregational Church, on the northeast corner of the center, dismantled their building in 1907, the First Christian Church purchased the lot for an estimated $300. The building was moved to the northeast corner of Routes 42 and 303 in 1916. Several additions were made after that time as seen in the c. 1930 photograph below. The building was demolished in 1962 when their new building on Route 303, just west of Towslee Elementary School, was completed. (Photograph courtesy of Brunswick United Methodist Church.)

This photograph shows the Brunswick Congregational Church. Although the congregation was formed in 1819, the church wasn't built until 1872, at a cost of $25,000; it was torn down in 1907. The bricks from this building were used in the new building, located on the southwest corner of Pearl and Center Roads. Two of the stained glass windows were purchased by the Methodist church and installed in 1916.

Bennett's Corners Community Methodist Church on West 130th Street in Hinckley is seen here in 1957. The congregation was formed in the 1840s, and the land was purchased in 1845 for $100 from John Hurd. The building was built in 1892. There have been many additions since that time. (Photograph courtesy of Bennett's Corners Community Methodist Church.)

The vault at Westview Cemetery is seen here in 1910. John Stearns donated the two acres of land that became Westview Cemetery.

This is the Beebetown Baptist Church in Liverpool Township. The wooden church was built in 1852 and remodeled in 1905, when it was covered with brick. (Photograph courtesy of Louise Varisco.)

Mt. Pleasant United Methodist Church was founded in 1873. Norman Chidsey provided the lumber from his farm to build the church. The church is located on the southwest corner of West 130th Street and Laurel Road. (Photograph courtesy of the Fuller family.)

This photograph shows the Town Line Cemetery on West 130th Street. (Photograph courtesy of the Fuller family.)

Four

SCHOOLS

School was first taught in Brunswick in a log cabin, with Sarah Tillotson as the first teacher. The first schoolhouse was built in 1817 just west of the center of town. During the rest of the 19th century, more primary schools were built throughout the township. This is Brunswick High School in 1893, two years after it was built.

The seventh graduating class of Brunswick High School was the class of 1906, which is seen in this photograph. The class size increased significantly from the first class of five in 1900. There are many familiar Brunswick names in this class. Pictured from left to right are: (bottom row) Herbert Tibbitts and Harold Barber; (second row) May Root (Damon), Lester Vaughan, Edna Woodard (Gibbs), and Elbridge Gibbs; (third row) John Ritchie, Mamie Codding (Waite), Harry Vaughan, and Dorothy Wood (Usher); (fourth row) Anna Johnson (Hadlock), Urban Sherman, Florence Woodard (Vaughan), and Coral Hunt; and (top row) Blake Somers, Calla Gibbs (Vaughan), and Carroll Damon. (Photograph courtesy of June Waite Kroupa.)

Center Primary School is seen here before the addition of a second room. It was located at 1246 Pearl Road across the street from where KFC is today. This building remained in use until August 1995 when it was destroyed by fire. A modern building was built around the original schoolhouse and was home to Family Pizza and Cheeter's Lounge when it burned.

Maude Evans was the teacher when this photograph of the Center Primary School was taken c. 1922. Pictured from left to right are: (first row) Dagmar Oehloff, Edna Ridiker, Margaret Bolles, Ellen Gibbs, unidentified, Geraldine Moxley, unidentified, Althea Vaughn, Lorraine Pimsner, Edna Reutter, and Caroline Oehloff; (second row) Emma Reuter, Dorothy Stebbins, and eight unidentified; and (third row) John Moxley, George Reutter, two unidentified, Adam Oehloff, Leonard Gibbs, ? Kling, and Homer Johnson. (Photograph courtesy of Ellen Gibbs.)

Horse drawn carts were the earliest "kid wagons" used to transport students to school. With the development of gasoline-powered engines, the school "truck," as seen here, replaced the horse-drawn wagon. In 1932, Brunswick used these two buses to transport 143 students to the center of town. (Photograph courtesy of Ward Bouman.)

The Bennett's Corners one-room schoolhouse, built in 1890, is seen here in the early 1900s. Following its use as a school, it became a town hall, and later, a community club used for plays and dances. As the building was used less and less during the 1950s after the advent of television, Rody Levandoski suggested it be given to the church. The condition of the donation of the community building to the church was that "community" be added to the church's name. Under the leadership of Myra Sanderson Slansky and Kenneth MacKenzie, the building was converted into a parsonage for the Bennett's Corner's Community Methodist Church. (Photograph courtesy of Rob Levandoski.)

This photograph captures a steam tractor moving the primary school building. During this time period, it was not uncommon for buildings to be moved, or torn down with the materials reused in a different structure. This is evidenced in the one-room schoolhouses that have been modified or added onto in Brunswick and are still in use as homes today.

Mamie Codding (Waite) is seen here c. 1906 during her first year of teaching at the Leinseder's Corners School. She taught here for two years before she was transferred to the Goodman's Corners Primary School in 1908. She took a test in Medina that allowed her to become a teacher. Her family lived several miles away on North Carpenter Road, so she had to board with another family that lived closer to Leinseder's Corners. (Photograph courtesy of June Waite Kroupa.)

The District No. 2 Primary School was located at Leinseder's Corners on the east side of Marks Road, north of Route 303. Students from Liverpool Township attended this school along with the Brunswick children. William Frank built the school in 1889 at a cost of $795.19. A stove was also purchased for the school for $13.

The District No. 7 schoolhouse is seen here in the winter of 1913. It was located at Laurel Road and South Carpenter, on the northeast corner.

This c. 1921–1922 photograph shows District schoolhouse No. 8, which was located at the corner of Substation and Grafton Roads. The teacher is Anna Bryenton. The students pictured are: (first row) Harry Pugli, Agnes Freese, Forrest Keller, Anna Toth, John Freese, Dorothy Hadlock, Elmer Gall, unidentified, and Charles Kling; (second row) Franklin Morton, unidentified, Louella Tibbitts, unidentified, Raymond Case, Ethel Brandt, Kathryn Vaughn, Almeda Morton, and Marion Kling.; and (third row) Herbert Reutter, Clarence Locke, Milliard James, Kenneth Balton, and Edson Peck. (Photograph courtesy of Forrest Keller.)

The children waited for the "kid wagon," and in later years, for the school bus, in this building. (Photograph courtesy of Forrest Keller.)

This coal house was used at the Street Car Stop 66 schoolhouse located on the southwest corner of Grafton and Substation Roads. (Photograph courtesy of Forrest Keller.)

This Goodman's Corners school picnic was held at the District No. 6 primary school *c.* 1890. This school was located on the northeast corner of North Carpenter and Grafton Roads. Mamie (nee Codding) Waite taught here for one year before she married Jesse Waite.

This house, located at 2195 Pearl Road, was converted from the District No. 4 schoolhouse to the residence it is today. It can be found on the east side of Pearl Road, just south of Sleepy Hollow.

Pictured here is Brunswick High School *c*. 1906, when Louie Brown was the teacher.

The 1910 Brunswick High School graduating class is pictured here inside the Brunswick Methodist Church. Bernice Freese was the valedictorian, and the class motto was "Yesterday, Today, and Tomorrow." (Photograph courtesy of Forrest Keller.)

This c. 1950s aerial view of the Brunswick School complex shows present-day Edwards Middle School in the foreground and Visintainer Middle School in the background. Edwards was built in 1921, with additions in 1925, 1955, 1958, and 1960. It was known as the "south house," and in 1949, the north house, which has received two additions was built. (Photograph courtesy of Rosemarie Skrletts Beyer.)

Mr. Maple, teacher at Brunswick High School, clowns with students Bob Eyssen, Paul Rumbaugh, and Ward Bowman c. 1932.

This photograph was taken from the first yearbook put together in Brunswick. It shows the faculty for all 12 grades in 1938. Pictured from left to right are: (front row) Miss Ogle, Miss Bramley, Miss Berhardy, and Miss Tinstman; and (back row) Mr. Corwin, Miss Gallagher, Superintendent of Brunswick Schools Mr. Detrow, Miss DePodesta, and Mr. Grills. (Photograph courtesy of Ethel Hemeyer Waite.)

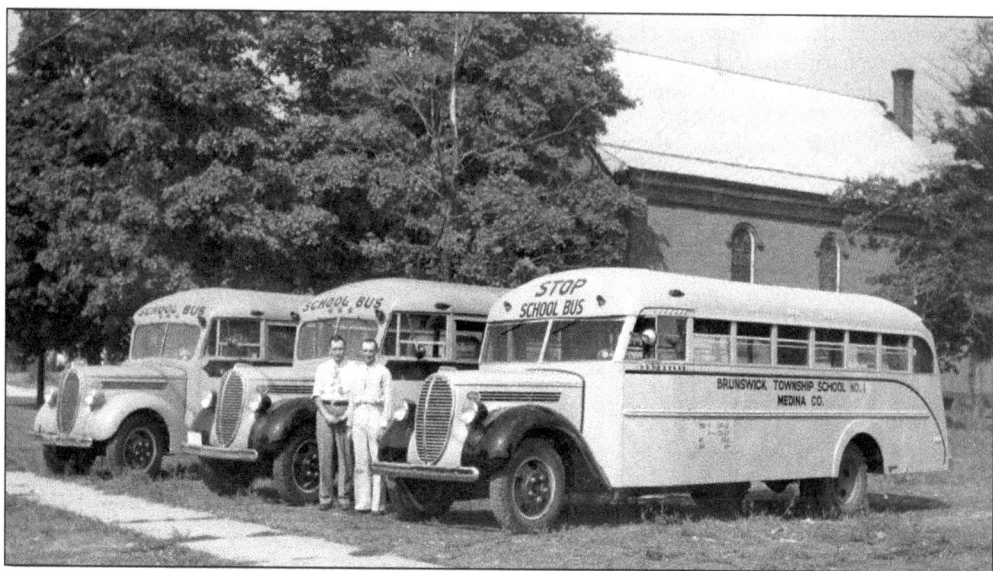

In 1939, Brunswick had three school buses. The drivers at that time were Corte Carlton, Harold Clement, and Tom Hogue. Pictured here are Corte Carlton and Otto Morlock with the Methodist Church in the background. (Photograph courtesy of Rose Carlton Miktuk.)

Pictured here are Brunswick High School Majorettes 1955–1956, left to right: Carol Widenmeyer, Lynda Barnes, head majorette Elaine Hanes, and Adele Neura. (Photograph courtesy of Albert Sego.)

Albert Sego's teaching career began in Brunswick in 1948. He spent nearly 30 years teaching instrumental music to the many students who passed through our schools. Mr. Sego led the band in many celebrations, concerts, parades, and football games here in Brunswick. (Photograph courtesy of Albert Sego.)

Pictured here c. 1960 are Brunswick school bus drivers Helen Chidsey (on the far left) and husband Myron Chidsey (second from the right). (Photograph courtesy Lori Chidsey Wagner.)

Towslee Elementary School faculty are pictured here on January 25, 1967. (Photograph courtesy of Rosemarie Skrletts Beyer.)

Marc Hunter was High School State Champion three times, once in cross-country and twice in track. He was "All American" in cross-country and track 10 times at Cleveland State University. His record 4:13 still stands in the mile at Brunswick. Seen here is the 1973–1974 cross-country team: (first row) Mike Bitting, Dan Cipullo, Matt Dillon, Jay Menke, Dan Laux, and Mike Faler; and (second row) Mike Berken, Harvey Baisden, Dale Laux, Marc Hunter, Mark Shick, Kerry Hunter, and Ted Dukles.

Five

HAPPENINGS

Homecoming celebrations and reunions have long been a tradition in Brunswick. They have continued through the years in one form or another, even through today. They are a time for family, friends, and neighbors to get together to share food and entertainment, and to catch up on news. Here is the Old Settler's Reunion that was held on August 13, 1910 at the Brunswick Methodist Church. (Photograph courtesy of Brunswick United Methodist Church.)

Pictured here is the 1934 Brunswick Homecoming.

Around 1900, the local play *13 Old Maids* was held at the Methodist Church. Some of the ladies pictured here include: Mrs. Somers, Mrs. Clement, Mrs. Johnson, Mrs. Livingston, Mrs. Babcock, Mrs. Strong, Mrs. Stebbins, Mrs. Tillotson, and Mrs. Perkins.

The Brunswick Community Band was a part of the July 4th parade and festivities. Director Jay Livingston is preparing the men's band. Pictured in this photograph are Hayden Morton, Eth Wyman, Ernie Wilkie, Harry Vaughn, Arthur Gardner, Carroll Damon, Verne Miner, Silas Ashdown, Walter Folley, Seeley Stebbins, Clare Cadnum, Carl Rau, and Harry Lincoln.

A number of big storms occurred in 1909. This photograph shows trees that were knocked down during a storm that hit Brunswick on July 16, 1909, leaving eight inches of hail and destroying many local crops.

Pictured here are World War I soldiers in 1918: Howard Chapman, Jack Gavlak, Earle Gibbs, and Handy Miner.

This photograph was taken during a parade held by the Brunswick residents in honor of our returning World War I soldiers on July 4th, 1919. Other festivities during the day included a picnic at noon, which was followed by entertainment and ended with fireworks.

Motorcyclists ready for a Brunswick parade c. 1914.

Everyone from the Brunswick area knows about the return of the buzzards to Hinckley each March 15th. The legend behind the buzzard's annual arrival in Hinckley is "the Great Hinckley Hunt," which took place on Christmas Eve of 1818. Supposedly, to protect their livestock and crops, early settlers organized a large-scale hunt. More than 600 men and boys from Hinckley Township and the surrounding area participated. That day, they killed 17 wolves, 21 bears, 300 deer, and many smaller animals. Legend has it that with the spring thaw, the stench was so great that the buzzards were attracted to the carcasses and have been returning every year since. Seen here is a view of Hinckley. (Photograph courtesy of June Waite Kroupa.)

This is a *c.* 1920s photograph of the farmwomen of Brunswick at a 4-H camp meeting at Camp Crag. The camp was located at Hinckley Ridge, near the Summit County line. Among the women pictured are Alice Gibbs, Min Pimsner, May (nee Root) Damon, and Calla (nee Gibbs) Vaughan. (Photograph courtesy of Kathryn Buschow.)

Y.M.C.A. Picture about 1916-17
Brunswick group about 4 rows back
Ray Brandt, Howard Chapman, Handy
Miner, Richard Reutter, Frank Reutter

This YMCA photograph dates back to 1916–1917. The Brunswick group is about four rows back and shows Ray Brandt, Howard Chapman, Handy Miner, Richard Reutter, Frank Reutter, and Roy Betsicover.

Seen here are three local baseball players with their dates on their way to a baseball game.

A community baseball game at Bennett's Corners is pictured here in the late 1920s. (Photograph courtesy of Rob Levandoski.)

This is a c. 1918 community baseball team. Less than 50 years after the Cincinnati Red Stockings became the first professional baseball team, these boys were playing the game locally. This Brunswick team is pictured from left to right: (front row) Perry Smith, Richard Reutter, Clare Cadnum, Howard Chapman, and Leo Root; and (back row) Lloyd Vaughn, Eddie Gibbs, Harry Lincoln, Earl Gibbs, Tom Armitage, and Verne Miner.

The Harmony Heavers, a Brunswick "jug band," are seen here in the late 1930s. Harold Chidsey is playing the jug, and Clyde Levandoski is playing the accordion. (Photograph courtesy of Rob Levandoski.)

Air races originated about 1909 in France. Airplanes followed a course of 10 to 15 miles guided by pylons. The National Air Races came to Cleveland in 1929 and continued through 1939, when World War II began; they resumed in 1946 and ended in 1949, when the Korean War began. Prior to World War II, grandstands were located along Brook Park Road, where NASA is now. Following World War II, the grandstands moved to a location in front of where the IX Center is today. The event, held on Labor Day Weekend, a precursor to today's Cleveland Air Show, was the largest event in the Cleveland area, drawing more than 200,000 people. Bob Swanson was qualifying *Full House* #80, his North American Mustang P-51, a fighter plane that cost $3,500. He was flying at 150 feet when the engine failed, and he crash-landed in a field along North Carpenter and Route 303 *(above)*. He was hoping to win the $16,000 for first place in the Thompson Trophy contest offered by Thompson Products (later TRW). Not giving up, Swanson obtained another plane from Texas, *Second Fiddle*. Even though it was without the modifications of *Full House*, he managed a fifth-place finish, which won him $2200. This was his last race. (c. 1946) (Photographs courtesy of June Waite Kroupa.)

Seen here, looking southwest, is a 1958 parade through the center of town with a Brownie troop participating. (Photograph courtesy of Rosemarie Skrletts Beyer.)

This is an aerial view of the Chamber of Commerce Homecoming. It was held at Visintainer/Edwards Middle School during the late 1950s to raise money for what would become Neura Park. Nationality Days replaced the Chamber's Homecoming, which was held at Laurel Square. Following Nationality Days, Old Fashioned Days began at Edwards before moving to the Brunswick High School Complex on Route 303. (Photograph courtesy of Albert Sego.)

Neura Park on Route 303 west is named after Captain Ted P. Neura Jr. Pictured in the top photograph is the dedication of the Vietnam Veterans Memorial Wall in Washington D.C. on November 12, 1982. Ted's mother Malvina (nee Pawlus) Neura is showing Captain Neura's photograph underneath his name. He was the first Medina County man killed in the Vietnam War in 1963. He graduated from Brunswick High School in 1951 and was a tackle on the high school football team. The Dedication Ceremony, when the plaque was erected at Neura Park, is seen in the bottom photograph. Pictured are: Ted's football coach, Bill Jacob, Jim Hayas, Brunswick school superintendent, and Ted's mother, Malvina Neura. (Photographs courtesy of Aqua Neura Witkowski.)

Minstrel shows were still deemed to be an acceptable form of entertainment. This one took place c. 1960 in the auditorium of Brunswick High School, which is now Edwards Middle School. (Photograph courtesy of Lori Chidsey Wagner.)

A local band, "The Mood Makers," performed at local functions. Pictured in the c. 1965–1966 photograph, from left to right, are Mike Beyer, Chuck Bell, Bruce Skrletts, and Rosemarie Skrletts Beyer. (Photograph courtesy of Rosemarie Skrletts Beyer.)

Among the many events that took place to celebrate Brunswick's sesquicentennial in 1965 was the parade. It was the largest in the history of Brunswick and lasted more than two hours. During the Sesquecentennial Celebration, men couldn't shave without a permit and ladies couldn't wear makeup without a permit. If they were caught doing so, it was the pokey for them, as seen above. (Photograph courtesy of Lori Chidsey Wagner.)

Howard and Velda (nee Drake) Chapman are pictured here at the Sesquicentennial Celebration in Brunswick in 1965. Velda Chapman, an artist, is seen with many of her paintings of local scenes. (Photograph courtesy of Grace Ruf.)

The fire and police station, west of the center, was dedicated on July 4, 1962. Corte Carleton is third from the left. (Photograph courtesy of Rose Carlton Miktuk.)

On July 20, 2003, the historical marker pictured here was dedicated. These special historical markers were awarded in conjunction with Ohio's year long bicentennial celebration. The dedication included tours of Heritage Farm Museum, a picnic, activities for children, and an unveiling ceremony. During the second weekend in October, Heritage Farm is humming with activity, as it is the setting for Heritage Days. There are numerous activities for everyone, including demonstrations of period craftsmanship, entertainment, a picnic, and a weekend-long Civil War encampment with reenactments. The reenactors are pictured here during the first annual Heritage Days. Heritage Days is a celebration of Brunswick's past and allows our citizens an opportunity to step back in time.

Six

FARMS AND FAMILIES

In 1815, the first settlers to arrive in Brunswick included Frederick and Solomon Deming, John Hulet, Seymour Chapin, John Stearns, Andrew Deming, and Henry Bogue, along with their families. Other familiar names of the early settlers were Samuel Tillotson, Ephraim Lindley, and Abraham Freese. The first homes were log cabins, followed by frame houses once the saw mills had been erected. This early Brunswick home was located on Route 303 west. It was built by Thomas Stearns and later was the residence of Abijah Stearns.

Grant and Rebecca (nee High) Tillotson are pictured here c. 1910. Grant attended Baldwin University in Berea, Ohio, for two terms. A farmer who bred Jersey cattle, Grant was a Methodist and a prohibitionist as well. Grant sold his farm to Clara and Elmer Eyssen in 1927 and lived in Medina until his death in 1937.

The Tillotson House is seen here c. 1930s when it was used as a fruit stand by the Eyssen family. Samuel and Sarah (nee Partridge) Tillotson arrived in Brunswick in 1815 from Massachusetts with their ten children. (Photograph courtesy of Bill Eyssen.)

This photograph of the Eyssen Farm dates to the 1930s. (Photograph courtesy of Bill Eyssen.)

The Eyssen Farm is pictured here during the 1920s. The Eyssens went on to establish Mapleside Farms, which today draws visitors from all over Ohio. It is also the home of the Johnny Appleseed Festival.

This is a 1940s photograph of Bill Eyssen and his father Elmer at the Eyssen Farm. (Photograph courtesy of Bill Eyssen.)

The Harold Clement House is seen here on Pearl Road. It was demolished in 2004.

The Lewis Peck house was located at Laurel and Substation Roads.

The Peck and Aylard families are pictured here from left to right: (front row) two unidentified, Nellie Aylard, unidentified, Mable James, Clara Peck, three unidentified, Ella Aylard, and unidentified; and (back row) unidentified, Wesley Peck, Lewis Peck, Emaline Aylard, Mrs. Peck (mother of Lewis), two unidentified, Carroll Damon, Eli Peck, unidentified, and Arthur Aylard.

The Damon Farm was located on Center Road. The Damons lived in Brunswick for 80 years. Carroll and Mae (nee Root) Damon were graduates of Brunswick High School in 1906, and both were teachers in the area as well. They farmed in Brunswick for 50 years, until the construction of Interstate 71 took their farm.

May (nee Root) and Carroll Damon are pictured here. (Photograph courtesy of June Waite Kroupa.)

The Neura homestead is seen here as it stood in 1920 on Substation Road. It was built about 1870 by George Barry Jr. The home and property were sold to Joseph Hall in 1898. A month later it was deeded to Albert Hall. In 1921, it was sold to Theodore Neura and remained in the Neura family until 2003. A movement is currently underway to save this old home, one of the few remaining in the Brunswick. (Photograph courtesy of Aqua Neura Witkowski.)

Malvina (nee Pawlus) and Theodore P. Neura are seen here at their wedding in the early 1920s. The couple was married at Neura's Grove. (Photograph courtesy of Aqua Neura Witkowski.)

This stately house stood on the northwest corner of Route 303 and Town Line Road, as it was once known (West 130th Street), and faced east. This intersection was known as Sherman's Corners. The brick one-and-a-half-story addition faced Route 303. Moses Sherman arrived in Brunswick in 1832. He was born in Newport, Rhode Island, in 1803. With his parents, he moved to New York in 1825 where he learned to be a cooper. The art of coopering dates back centuries. Coopers made casks, or barrels, as well as pails, dippers, and churns. The casks held everything from gunpowder to milk. He became a farmer upon his arrival in Brunswick. He lived at this home until his death in 1882. (Photograph courtesy of Jeff Lanphear.)

This photograph, taken at Eagle Cliff, is of the Sherman Family, left to right, as follows: (seated) Sarah (nee Sherman) Babcock, Byron Sherman, Olive Sherman, and Martha Sherman; and (standing) Delazon Sherman, Stephen Sherman, and Moses Sherman. (Photograph courtesy of Jeff Lanphear.)

This is Urban Sherman.

Charles and Mertie Sherman's house is shown here. (Photograph courtesy of Jeff Lanphear.)

A typical snow storm in Brunswick showers the Waite family home on North Carpenter in the 1940s. (Photograph courtesy of June Waite Kroupa.)

Jesse and Mamie (nee Codding) Waite are seen here at their 50th Wedding Anniversary on November 6, 1959. (Photograph courtesy of June Waite Kroupa.)

This photograph shows men threshing wheat at the Waite farm, which was located on the east side of North Carpenter Road, just south of Boston Road.

The Daniel Stow home was located at 565 Pearl Road and was built in the mid-1850s.

The Chapman house is seen here on Route 303, where Arby's is today, in front of the high school complex and Towslee Elementary School. Mrs. Elza (nee Newton) Chapman is pictured with her children Howard and Myrtle. (Photograph courtesy of Grace Ruf.)

Eliza "Elza" (nee Newton) and Theo Chapman. (Photograph courtesy of Grace Ruf.)

Myrtle Chapman (Ruf), age five, is seen here *c.* 1905 with her grandmother Ellen Newton. This photograph was a prized possession of Myrtle's. (Photograph courtesy of Grace Ruf.)

The Chapman barn and silo is seen here. The Chapman farm was located on Route 303 where Brunswick High School and Towslee Elementary School are today. (Photograph courtesy of Grace Ruf.)

Mr. Drake is seen seated on the left with Ellen Newton on the right. Nora (nee Newton) Brasse is behind her mother Ellen. The others are the children and spouses of John and Nora Brasse, pictured when the family lived at the corner of Route 303 and Gary Boulevard. (Photograph courtesy of Grace Ruf.)

This *c.* 1886 photograph shows Mr. and Mrs. Charles Drake of Strongsville who lived at Bennett's Corners. (Photograph courtesy of Grace Ruf.)

This Chapman family portrait pictures, from left to right, as follows: (bottom row) Mildred, Mabel, and Elizabeth; and (top row) Richard, George, Mary Jane, Theo, Will, Jenny, and Lon. (Photograph courtesy of Grace Ruf.)

The Newton family is pictured here left to right: (bottom row) James, Eliza, and Ellen; and (top row) Nora, Ray, Clara, and Earl. (Photograph courtesy of Grace Ruf.)

Pictured here on their wedding day, May 10, 1910, is, left to right: (bottom row) Elbridge Gibbs and Edna Woodard and (top row) Callista Gibbs (sister of Elbridge) and Harry Vaughan. (Photograph courtesy of Kathryn Buschow.)

This portrait commemorated the 50th anniversary of Callista (nee Gibbs) and Harry Vaughan and Elbridge and Edna (nee Woodard) Gibbs. (Photograph courtesy of Kathryn Buschow.)

The William Vaughan family is pictured at their farm on what today is Hadcock Road. (Photograph courtesy of Kathryn Buschow.)

The Gibbs farm was on the east side of Substation just north of Route 303 and the interurban station. Members of the Gibbs family c. 1912 included, from left to right: (bottom row) Earle, Edward, Farnum, Calla (nee Gibbs) Vaughan holding daughter Kathryn, Ellen (nee Blakeslee) Gibbs, Roe Moxley holding John Moxley, and Nellie Moxley; and (top row) Harry Vaughan holding Althea, Geraldine Moxley, Esther Gibbs, standing child Clara Moxley, Harry Lincoln, Anna (nee Gibbs) Lincoln, Ellen Gibbs, unidentified, and Elbridge Gibbs holding Janet. The automobile in the photograph is a Samson. (Photograph courtesy of Ellen Gibbs.)

The B.W. Freese home is located on Route 303 west. (Photograph courtesy of Walt Wozniak.)

Orson E. and Jane E. (nee Somers) Harrington are pictured here. Jane was born in 1845 to parents Elmina (nee Freese) and Elijah Somers, who was a local physician. Orson Harrington is from an old Columbia Station family. Jane Somers was the granddaughter of B.W. Freese, whose brother was Abraham Freese. (Photograph courtesy of Walt Wozniak.)

Hazel and William Morton are seen at their farm, which was on the northwest corner of Route 303 and Substation Road. This is also the location of the old William Dragy Farm. (Photograph courtesy of Forrest Keller.)

Despite all the hard work on a farm in Brunswick in 1930, there was still time for fun. Karl Ruf is seen with his sister Alice on the Ruf Farm on North Carpenter Road. (Photograph courtesy of Grace Ruf.)

The Lewis W. Fuller house on the Fuller farm is seen here in the late 1800s. The Fuller Farm encompassed over 400 acres, stretching from West 130th Street to Carpenter Road south of Sleepy Hollow. Members of the Fuller family still live on the property today. (Photograph courtesy of the Fuller family.)

Earl Page Fuller and his wife Nellie (nee Ashdown) are pictured here. Nellie arrived in the Brunswick area in 1913 with her family, who emigrated from England. She lived to be 103, and both she and Earl are buried in the Town Line Cemetery on West 130th Street. (Photograph courtesy of the Fuller family.)

Pictured in this early 1900s Fuller family photo are, from left to right: Earl Page Fuller; Earl's brother Gene with his wife Lydia (nee Graf, from Abbeyville)and their children; unidentified; Lewis W., father of Earl and Gene; and the housekeeper. (Photograph courtesy of the Fuller family.)

This photograph was taken on Charlie Leinseder's farm, which was located north of where KFC is today. (Photograph courtesy of Forrest Keller.)

Pictured above is a birthday party celebration at the Livingston's in July of 1942. Pictured left to right are: (bottom row) Jay Livingston, unidentified, and Bessie (nee Freese) Keller (also pictured below); and (standing) Bessie Livingston, unidentified, and Bert Keller. The Livingston farmstead was located on the north side of Route 303 east of where Hadcock Road is today, approximately where Brunswick Oncology is located today. (Photographs courtesy of Forrest Keller.)

Seen here is the Stebbins family at their home at 765 Pearl Road. The house is still standing today, although the exterior has changed. Pictured left to right are: (seated) W.B. Stebbins and Mary Stebbins Pritchard; and (standing) Seely Stebbins (son of W.B.) and his mother Margaret Stebbins. (Photograph courtesy of Ellen Gibbs.)

The Cowles Farm was located on Boston Road east of where the Forrest Hills development is today. (Photograph courtesy of June Waite Kroupa.)

Alice and Watson Carpenter are pictured here. They lived on North Carpenter Road. (Photograph courtesy of Grace Ruf.)

The farmstead of Peter and Mary Groenig was located at 4613 Laurel Road *c.* 1947. Today this is the home of Heritage Farm Museum and the Brunswick Area Historical Society.

This picture of Bernice Freese was taken at the home of Henry and Mary Freese located at the corner of Grafton and Substation Roads where the Brunswick Hills Police Station is today. Bernice Freese was a Brunswick school teacher and married Bert Keller. Bernice's great-grandfather, Abraham Freese, surveyed Brunswick Township prior to the War of 1812. Abraham and his sons settled in Brunswick in 1817 at the corner of Grafton and Substation Roads. (Photograph courtesy of Forrest Keller.)

The Keller Family, pictured left to right, included: (top row) Bert, Forrest, and Bernice (nee Freese); and (bottom row) Bessie. The Keller farm was located where the Pepperwood Estates development is, on the south side of Grafton Road between Route 42 and Substation Road. (Photograph courtesy of Forrest Keller.)

Grant, Bertha, and Elbert Chidsey are pictured at the Chidsey farm *c*. 1910. (Photograph courtesy of Lori Chidsey Wagner.)

The Chidsey Farm is pictured here around the turn of the last century. (Photograph courtesy of Lori Chidsey Wagner.)

Horatio Chidsey is seen here driving a horse-drawn wagon. Horatio John Chidsey was the son of Norman Chidsey and Jane Wilson Eaton who were married in 1826. Of six children, the first died, and the others were Charlotte, Truman, Horatio, Minnie, and Eliza. They lived on South Town Line (West 130th Street) on what was known as the Kennedy Farm. Horatio married Janetta "Nett" Ruth Greenwood in 1857, and Horatios' brother, Truman married Janetta's sister, Janetta Betsy Ann Greenwood in 1858. Horatio and his wife had two children, Lucien and Mary, who married Edgar Benjamin. Note the leather fly net that is draped over the horses, shaking with the horses' movement to keep the flies away. (Photograph courtesy of the Benjamin family.)

This home located at 2050 West 130th Street was built in 1835 by Norman Chidsey, Eliza Chidsey Kennedy's father. Phil Kennedy, Norman's son-in-law, was standing in the front yard when he was told that Abraham Lincoln had been shot.

Grant Chidsey built this home, located at 1748 South Carpenter Road. Many additions have been made over the years. (Photograph courtesy Waite & Son Funeral Homes.)

Shown here is Myron Chidsey with one of his prize-winning Jerseys. Myron's father, Grant, purchased a yearling bull for a record $2,000 in 1919. He was well known for his herd of dairy cattle, one of the finest in the United States, and in 1932, Chidsey's champion Jersey, Torono's Fern Lass, won a national gold medal. (Photograph courtesy of Lori Chidsey Wagner.)

Albert I. Root's home was located on the east side of Pearl Road across from the Center Primary schoolhouse. (Photograph courtesy of Ellen Gibbs.)

May Root (Damon) is pictured here c. 1906 with her parents Albert and Anna (nee Blakeslee) Root. Albert served as a Township Clerk in Brunswick. (Photograph courtesy of Ellen Gibbs.)

This daguerreotype shows Edgar Benjamin and his sister on the Benjamin Farm on West 130th Street. (Photograph courtesy of the Benjamin family.)

In this *c.* 1914 photograph, Elmer Benjamin is in the wagon being pulled by his cousin. (Photograph courtesy of the Benjamin family.)

This photograph shows a 1950s aerial view of the Benjamin Farm on West 130th Street. (Photograph courtesy of the Benjamin family.)

The Benjamin family is pictured here c. 1912–1913, from left to right: Alice Loe holding Elmer Benjamin, Mary (nee Chidsey) Benjamin, and Alice Chidsey. (Photograph courtesy of the Benjamin family.)

The home of Sarah (nee Sherman) and George Byron Babcock is seen here, with George holding daughter Constance (Smith), and Erma Bradley far right. (Photograph courtesy of Jeff Lanphear.)

The Babcock home was located on the northwest corner of Routes 303 and 42. Frank and Carrie Babcock did not have any children, but many of the local schoolteachers were boarders at their home. Pictured here, left to right, are teacher Nina Cole, Carrie Babcock, teacher Harriet Simmons, and Frank Babcock. (Photograph courtesy of Forrest Keller.)

This is Dr. George Pitkin's home c. 1915 when it stood on Pearl Road on the north side of the Brunswick Plaza. The house was built about 1860. George Pitkin was the local funeral director. At that time, services were held either in church or the family's home. It wasn't until the 1960s that the Carlson family went into business in Brunswick and opened Carlson Funeral Home. A.B. Clark later moved this house to 1589 Jefferson Street where it still stands today.

Pictured here c. 1912–1913 are four generations of an old Bennett's Corners family: left to right, Ruby (nee Warner) Levandoski, her grandfather Henry Warner, her father Alfred Warner, and Ruby's baby son, Corwin. (Photograph courtesy of Rob Levandoski.)

The Ferriman house stands at the location where Seymour Knox arrived and settled in 1821, on Sleepy Hollow Road. Seymour Knox was originally from Blandford, Massachusetts, and purchased the property in 1818.

Pictured here are: (top row) Nellie (nee Knox) Ferriman, Ray Ferriman, and William Ferriman (son of Holden and Nancy (Burgess) Ferriman); and (bottom row) Neil Ferriman. Nellie was a schoolteacher before her marriage to William. Nellie is the granddaughter of Seymour Knox. Her family can be traced back to Edward Doty of the *Mayflower* through her grandmother, Betsey Doty. (Photograph courtesy of Pat Van Hoose.)

The Gerspacher farm was located on Route 303 and North Carpenter Road *c.* 1960s. In the early 1970s, the home was moved to North Carpenter Road, where it still stands today, to make way for the K-mart Plaza. Seen below is the sugar house that was on the farm. (Photographs courtesy Waite & Son Funeral Homes.)

Brunswick Center is seen here in the summer of 2004. Very few remnants of our past remain; only Brunswick United Methodist Church, the red brick office building across the street, and Westview Cemetery. The one-lane mud roads, the circle, and the old schoolhouses are long gone. Only the headstones of the first settlers remain as a reminder of our forbearers and the struggles and triumphs in their settlement of what has become our home. (Photograph courtesy Gary Werner.)

Visit us at
arcadiapublishing.com

www.ingramcontent.com/pod-product-compliance
Lightning Source LLC
Chambersburg PA
CBHW080603110426
42813CB00006B/1394